1. MORE THAN JUST A ~~~

Text by Barbara Cooper

Illustrations by Maggie Raynor

Series consultant: Valerie Watson

Compass Equestrian

© Compass Equestrian Limited 1996
Setting by HGJ
Origination by Dot Gradations
Printed in England by Westway Offset
ISBN 1 900667 00 2

British Library Cataloguing in Publication Data.
A catalogue record for this book is available from the British Library.

There are many kinds of pet.

Some are cuddly.

Some are not.

Some can run fast.

Some can hardly walk.

Some are noisy.

Some are silent.

Some will climb all over you

Some just sit around doing nothing.

All pets have to be cared for, but they are not really much trouble, and most of them take up very little space.

GEORGE

3

A pony is more than just a pet. He can be as much part of a family and as much loved as a dog or a cat or a rabbit or a guinea pig.

But he costs a lot more to keep, needs a lot more looking after and takes up a lot more space.

You cannot leave him alone all day without keeping an eye on him. You cannot take him in the car when you go out. And when you go on holiday you must leave him with someone who knows how to look after him.

However, a pony can be a lot more fun to be with than an ordinary pet. He is much stronger and can pull a cart full of people or other heavy loads for a long way and a long time.

He can be as much of a friend and companion as a
dog, but, most important of all, he can carry a
human — such as you — on his back.
Before it is safe for you to handle a pony, there are a
lot of things you must learn about him.

The different parts of ponies and horses are
known as 'points'. Some of them are the
same as parts of your own body; others can
only be found on ponies and horses, and
they have special names.

LOINS-

HIND
QUARTERS

TAIL

HOCK

STIFLE

FL

FETL

PAST

HO

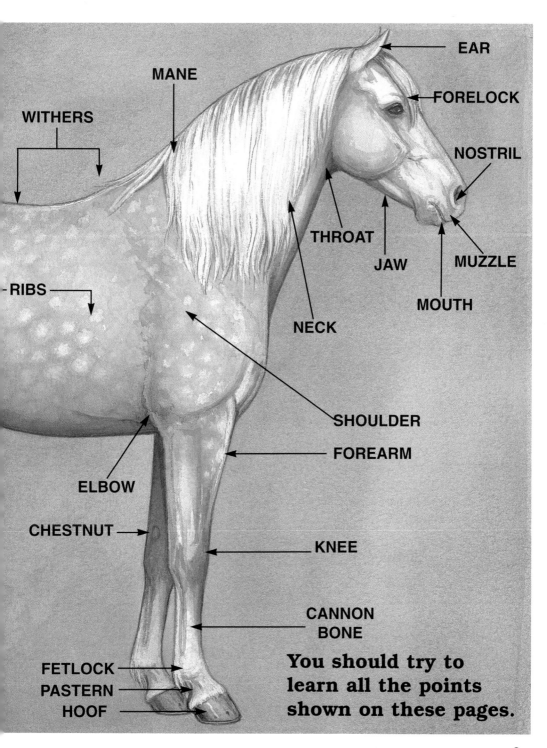

EAR

MANE

FORELOCK

WITHERS

NOSTRIL

THROAT

JAW

MUZZLE

MOUTH

RIBS

NECK

SHOULDER

FOREARM

ELBOW

CHESTNUT

KNEE

CANNON
BONE

**You should try to
learn all the points
shown on these pages.**

FETLOCK

PASTERN

HOOF

Now you need to know what makes
a pony's shape. You may never have
dreamed that your shape and his
come from the same design.
But look at the pictures on these
two pages.

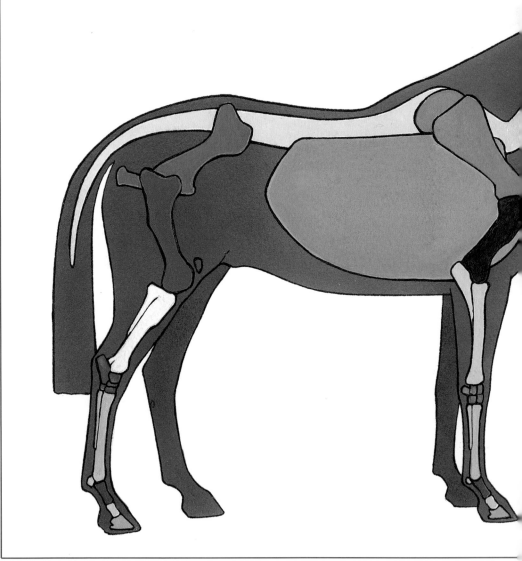

You can see that the pony's hock and knee joints (coloured brown) are the same as your ankles and wrists. His lower legs (light blue) are the same as the bones in your feet and hands. The bones in the pony's pasterns (red and yellow) are the same as your finger bones, and his feet (green) are the same as your finger-tips.

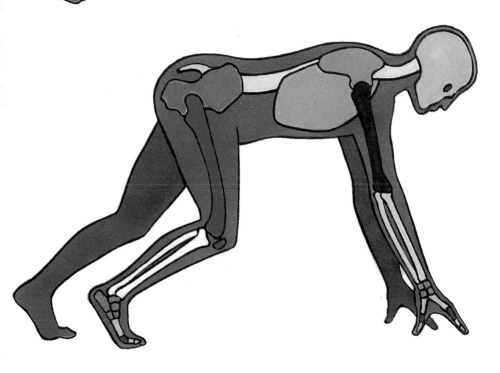

Ponies are smaller than horses. You can tell the difference by measuring their height. The measure is called a 'hand' because in the old days men actually used the width of their hands to measure a pony or a horse from the ground to his withers (which is the highest point on his back.) A man's hand is generally around 4 inches or 10 centimetres wide. Today we use special measuring sticks to work out the height. Ponies are no more than 58 inches (147 centimetres) or 14 hands 2 inches high.

The smallest pony and the tallest dog, the St Bernard, are almost the same size. But you can't look after a pony in the same way as a dog.

You can buy dog and cat food in tins at the supermarket but a pony has to eat fresh grass in a field and needs hay — which is dried grass — in the winter as well.

A cat will live for about eighteen years, a dog for fourteen, mice and rats for only a year or two. These pets will be with you for the whole of their lives. A pony, however, can live for as long as

thirty years. By the age of four he will be fully grown, but you will go on growing until you are in your late teens. So the pony on whom you learn to ride when you are very young will be too small for you after two or three years and, sadly, you will probably have to sell him.

A cat can roam freely and will come home for her supper when she chooses but a pony has to be kept safely shut in his field or stable, and he depends on his owner to look after him all the time.

As you can see, there is a lot more to looking after a pony than just keeping an ordinary pet. There is also a lot more to riding than just sitting on a pony's back. Before you can become a really good rider you will need to understand how a pony thinks, how he feels, why he behaves in certain ways, what he can — and what he can't — do for you, how to make him happy and most important of all, how to be his best friend.

The next book in this series tells you what goes on in a pony's head.

2. HEAD FIRST